Grand Canyon
National Park

by Mike Graf

Reading Consultant:
Dr. Robert Miller
Professor of Special Education
Minnesota State University, Mankato

Bridgestone Books
an imprint of Capstone Press
Mankato, Minnesota

Bridgestone Books are published by Capstone Press
151 Good Counsel Drive, P.O. Box 669, Mankato, Minnesota 56002
http://www.capstone-press.com

Library of Congress Cataloging-in-Publication Data
Graf, Mike.
  Grand Canyon National Park / by Mike Graf.
  p. cm.—(National parks)
  Includes bibliographical references and index.
  Summary: Describes the Grand Canyon National Park, including its location, history,
plants and animals, weather, and activities for visitors.
  ISBN 0-7368-1375-6 (hardcover)
  1. Grand Canyon National Park (Ariz.)—Juvenile literature. [1. Grand Canyon National
Park (Ariz.) 2. National parks and reserves.] I. Title. II. National parks (Mankato, Minn.)
F788 .G73 2003
917.91'32—dc21   2001008092

Editorial Credits
Blake A. Hoena, editor; Karen Risch, product planning editor; Linda Clavel, designer; Anne
  McMullen, illustrator; Alta Schaffer, photo researcher

Photo Credits
Christian Heeb/Gnass Photo Images, cover, 1
Corbis, 18
Eda Rogers, 12
Jim Baron/The Image Finders, 6, 14, 16
Rankin Harvey/Houserstock, 17
Tom Till, 4, 8, 10

1 2 3 4 5 6 07 06 05 04 03 02

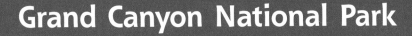

Grand Canyon National Park

In 1919, the U.S. government set aside land for the Grand Canyon National Park. The government creates national parks to protect natural areas such as the Grand Canyon. People are not allowed to hunt or build on national park lands. But the parks are open for people to visit and enjoy.

The Grand Canyon is one of the world's largest canyons. The Colorado River flows through it for 277 miles (446 kilometers). The canyon is up to 18 miles (29 kilometers) wide. Some areas of the canyon are more than 1 mile (1.6 kilometers) deep.

Grand Canyon National Park is located in northwestern Arizona. The park covers more than 1,900 square miles (4,900 square kilometers) of land.

Almost 5 million people visit Grand Canyon National Park each year. People go to view its scenery and wildlife. They hike and raft in the park. People also can visit the remains of an 800-year-old American Indian village at the Tusayan Museum.

The Grand Canyon is one of the largest canyons in the world.

The Colorado River starts in the Rocky Mountains. Its rushing waters helped create the Grand Canyon.

The Grand Canyon is about 5 million years old. But scientists believe that the dark rock at the bottom of the canyon is almost 2 billion years old. This rock is the base of a very old mountain range. Over time, the Colorado River has dug deep into the earth. It eroded away many layers of dirt and rock to uncover the dark rock.

Other forces help shape the Grand Canyon. Ice freezes in the cracks of rocks during winter. The ice causes the rocks to break apart. Rain washes dirt and rock down the canyon's slopes and into the river. These forces cause the canyon to widen.

Erosion has created many interesting features in the canyon. Toroweap Overlook is a 3,000-foot (900-meter) cliff that overlooks the Colorado River. Streams flowing down the canyon's steep slopes form waterfalls such as Havasu Falls.

Erosion has uncovered many layers of rock in the Grand Canyon.

People in the Grand Canyon

People have lived in and around the Grand Canyon for more than 10,000 years. Old American Indian sites can be found throughout the park. Hopi, Navajo, Havasupai, Hualapai, and Paiute Indians still live near the park.

In 1869, John Wesley Powell led a group of explorers through the Grand Canyon. Powell mapped the canyon. He named many of the canyon's features, including Bright Angel Creek and Sockdolager Rapids.

In the late 1800s, miners came to the Grand Canyon. The miners were looking for gold. But they found only copper and a gray mineral called asbestos. The miners used American Indian trails to travel through the canyon. Tourists now use some of these trails to hike in the park.

In 1901, the first railroad leading to the Grand Canyon was built. This railroad took tourists to the canyon's South Rim.

Some American Indians stored food in shelters they built in the side of the canyon's walls.

Weather

The park has three main areas. The North Rim is on the north side of the Colorado River. It rises 7,500 to 9,000 feet (2,290 to 2,740 meters) above sea level. Because of its height, the North Rim has cool weather. The average summer temperature is 75 degrees Fahrenheit (24 degrees Celsius). The North Rim also receives more rain and snow than other areas of the park. It receives about 30 inches (76 centimeters) of precipitation each year.

The South Rim is about 1,000 feet (300 meters) lower than the North Rim. Its average summer temperature is about 10 degrees Fahrenheit (5.7 degrees Celsius) warmer than the North Rim. The South Rim receives half as much precipitation as the North Rim.

Inside the canyon, the weather is hot and dry. Summer temperatures can be more than 100 degrees Fahrenheit (38 degrees Celsius) at the bottom of the canyon. This area also receives little rain.

Snow rarely falls at the bottom of the Grand Canyon.

The North Rim of the Grand Canyon receives a great deal of rain and snow. The precipitation allows a thick forest of aspen, spruce, and fir trees to grow.

The canyon's South Rim is drier. The type of trees that grow along the south side of the Colorado River need less water. These trees include oak, pine, and juniper trees.

Ponderosa pines grow on both rims of the canyon. They are the tallest trees in the park. They can grow to be more than 100 feet (30 meters) tall.

The bottom of the canyon usually is hot and dry. But willow, mesquite, and cottonwood trees grow near water.

Many other plants grow in and around the Grand Canyon. Several kinds of cactus grow in the canyon's hot, dry areas. Banana yucca plants also grow in the park. American Indians ate the yucca's fruit. They also used this plant to make soap, rope, and sandals.

Cactuses grow throughout the Grand Canyon.

Animals

Grand Canyon National Park is home to many mammals, birds, and reptiles. Desert bighorn sheep live on rocky slopes inside the canyon. Mule deer roam throughout the park. Many squirrels and beavers also live in the area.

Predators such as coyotes, bobcats, mountain lions, and ringtails hunt in the park. Ringtails are foxlike animals that have long tails with black and white rings.

Birds such as ravens, chickadees, and nuthatches nest in and around the canyon. Peregrine falcons and bald eagles are two rare birds that can be seen around the park.

Many snakes live in the canyon. Gopher snakes are common along the canyon's rims. The Grand Canyon pink rattlesnake can be found only in the Grand Canyon. This venomous snake sometimes makes a rattling noise with its tail when in danger.

Bighorn sheep are able to climb steep, rocky slopes.

Activities

Park visitors can hike, ride mules, or raft in the canyon. The park has many hiking trails. Visitors ride mules on guided trips to the bottom of the canyon. At Lees Ferry, people begin guided rafting trips down the Colorado River.

The National Park Service provides guided tours. Park rangers take visitors on walks through different parts of the park. They tell people about the park's features and wildlife.

Safety

Many people hike down into the canyon. But it is easier to hike into the canyon than it is to climb out. People should take their time while hiking to avoid becoming tired. Hikers also need to drink plenty of water. The heat in the canyon can cause people to become dehydrated.

While hiking or camping, park visitors should watch where they put their hands and feet. Snakes and scorpions live under rocks.

Park Issues

Several issues face Grand Canyon National Park. One problem is overcrowding. Millions of people visit the park each year. Large crowds can make the park less enjoyable for some visitors. They also make it more difficult to protect the park's natural beauty. People must be careful not to damage wildlife while hiking or camping. Visitors need to carry all of their garbage out of the park.

No dams exist within the park. But two nearby dams affect the flow of the Colorado River. At the upper end of the canyon, the Glen Canyon Dam forms Lake Powell. The Hoover Dam forms Lake Mead at the canyon's lower end.

These dams affect wildlife habitats in the area. They change the flow of the fast-moving waters in which some fish live. Bird habitats along the river have been flooded because of the lakes. Officials are discussing whether or not to remove the Glen Canyon Dam.

Glen Canyon Dam is at the northeast end of the park.

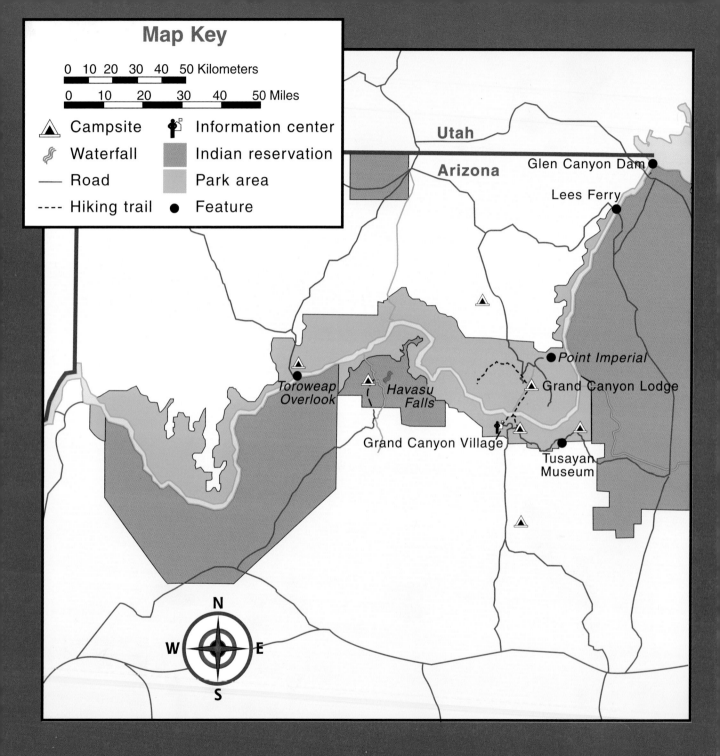

Map Key

0 10 20 30 40 50 Kilometers

0 10 20 30 40 50 Miles

△ Campsite

🛈 Information center

〰 Waterfall

Indian reservation

— Road

Park area

---- Hiking trail

● Feature

Utah

Arizona

Glen Canyon Dam ●

Lees Ferry ●

△

● Point Imperial

Toroweap Overlook ●

△ *Havasu Falls*

△ Grand Canyon Lodge

🛈 △ △

Grand Canyon Village

● Tusayan Museum

△

N

W **E**

S

Map Activity

The shortest distance between two places is a straight line. But the Grand Canyon is wide and has steep walls. Because of these features, no bridges or roads cross the Colorado River within the park. See how the canyon's shape affects the distance you travel from place to place in the park.

What You Need
Ruler
20-inch (51-centimeter) piece of string

What You Do
1. Find a campsite on the map. Then find a site you would like to visit. For example, Point Imperial is one of the highest areas in the park.
2. Using the ruler, measure the distance between the campsite and the place you picked to visit. Use the scale in the map's key to find out how far this distance is in miles (kilometers).
3. Next, measure the distance you would have to travel. Place one end of the string on your campsite. Then lay the string down, following roads, until you reach the place you picked to visit. Measure the length of string needed. What is the distance in miles (kilometers)?

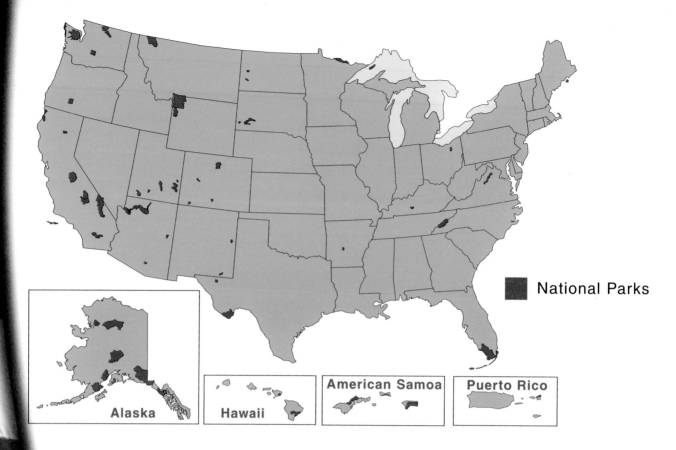

National Parks

Alaska

Hawaii

American Samoa

Puerto Rico

About National Parks

The U.S. government creates national parks to protect special natural areas. These parks allow everyone to enjoy such areas as the Grand Canyon. People can camp, hike, and view the wildlife and the scenery in national parks. But they are not allowed to hunt or build on park lands. The government set aside land for Grand Canyon National Park in 1919. Today, the United States has more than 50 national parks.

Words to Know

asbestos (ass-BESS-tuhss)—a gray mineral used to make fireproof material

dehydrated (dee-HYE-dray-tid)—not having enough water

erosion (ee-ROH-zhuhn)—the wearing away of land by water or wind

mammal (MAM-uhl)—a warm-blooded animal with a backbone; female mammals feed milk to their young.

precipitation (pree-sip-i-TAY-shuhn)—the rain and snow an area receives

predator (PRED-uh-tur)—an animal that hunts other animals for food

sea level (SEE LEV-uhl)—the average surface level of the world's oceans

venomous (VEN-uh-muhss)—having or producing a poison called venom; some snakes are venomous.

Read More

Meister, Cari. *Grand Canyon.* Going Places. Minneapolis: ABDO & Daughters, 2000.

Raatma, Lucia. *Our National Parks.* Let's See. Minneapolis: Compass Point Books, 2002.

Weintraub, Aileen. *The Grand Canyon: The Widest Canyon.* Great Record Breakers in Nature. New York: PowerKids Press, 2001.

Useful Addresses

Grand Canyon National Park
P.O. Box 129
Grand Canyon, AZ 86023

National Park Service
1849 C Street NW
Washington, DC 20240

Internet Sites

Grand Canyon Explorer—The Geology of the Grand Canyon
http://www.kaibab.org/geology/gc_geol.htm
National Park Service—Grand Canyon National Park
http://www.nps.gov/grca
U.S. National Parks Net—Grand Canyon National Park
http://www.grand.canyon.national-park.com

Index

American Indian, 5, 9, 13
animals, 5, 15, 16, 17, 19
Colorado River, 5, 7, 11, 13, 16, 19
dams, 19
erosion, 7
hiking, 5, 9, 16, 17, 19
miners, 9
mules, 16

North Rim, 11, 13
plants, 13
Powell, John Wesley, 9
rafting, 5, 16
railroad, 9
Rocky Mountains, 7
safety, 17
South Rim, 9, 11, 13
weather, 7, 11, 13, 17